MW00561787

THIS NOTEBOOK BELONGS TO

CONTACT

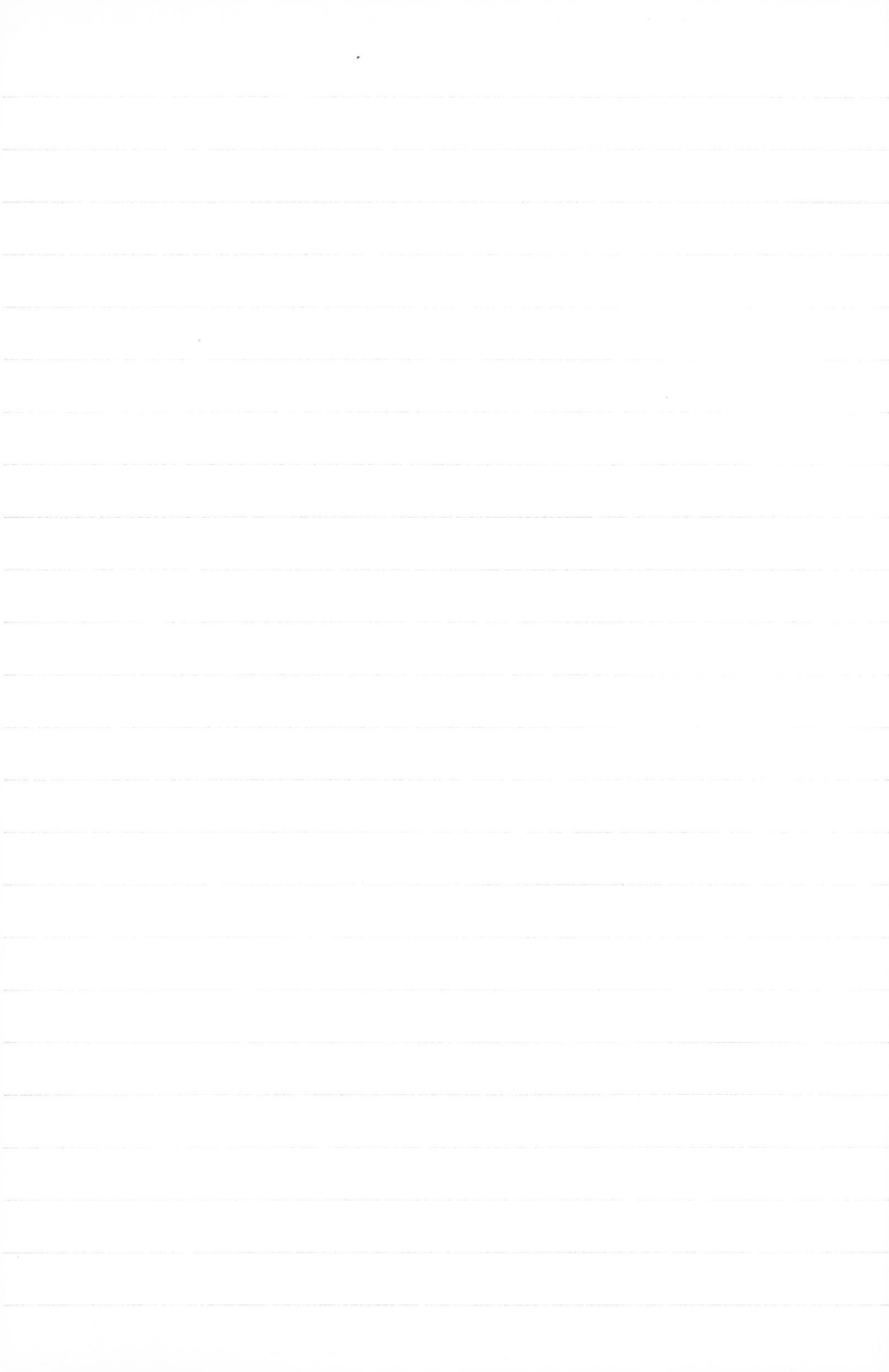

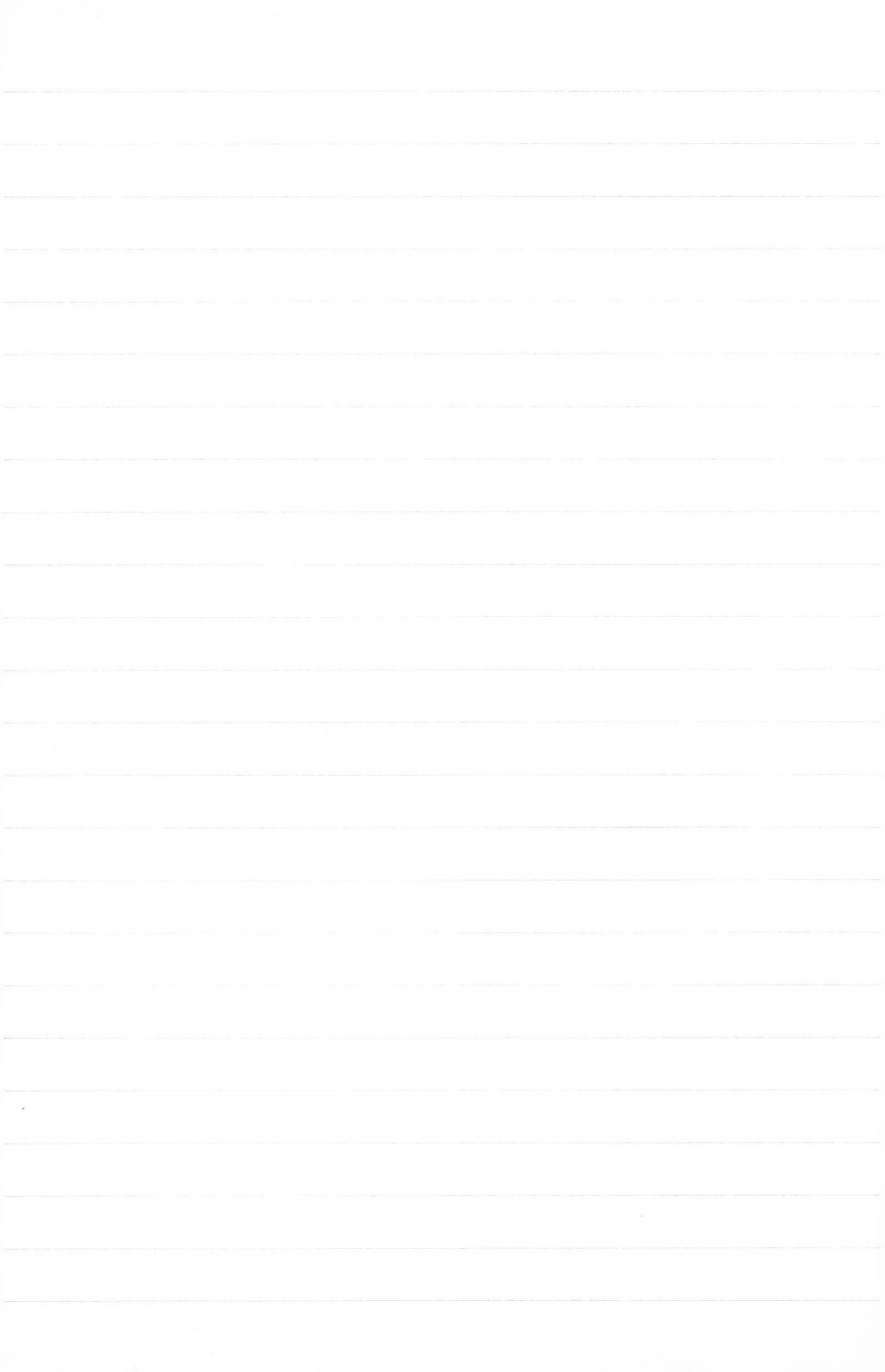

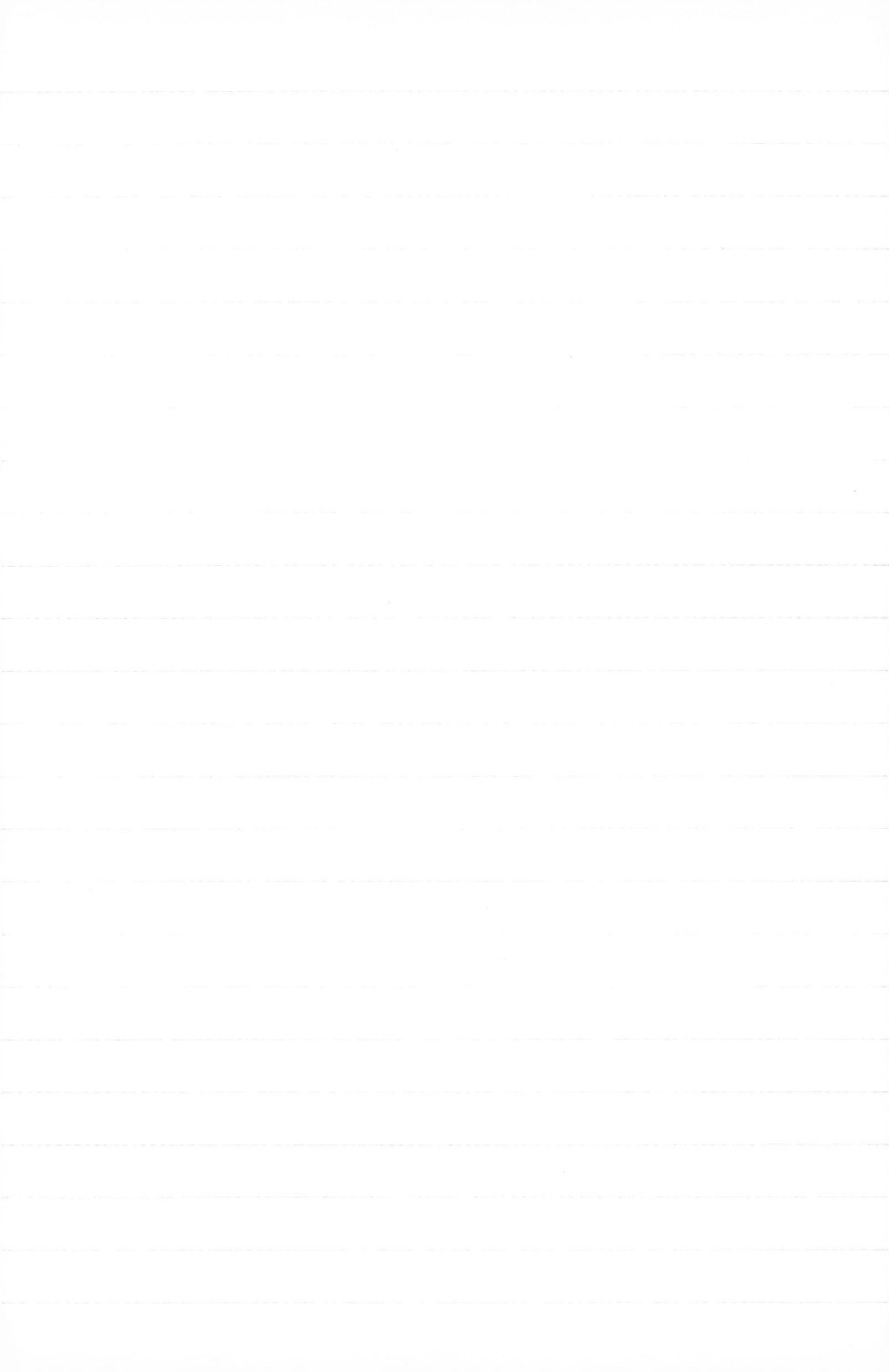

See our range of fine, illustrated books, ebooks, notebooks and art calendars:
www.flametreepublishing.com

This is a **FLAME TREE NOTEBOOK**
Published and © copyright 2023 Flame Tree Publishing Ltd

FTNB332 • 978-1-80417-353-4

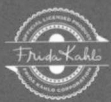

Frida Kahlo: Dark Pink
© 2023 Frida Kahlo Corporation/Licensed by www.artaskagency.com

One of the most iconic artists of the 20th century, Frida Kahlo's
bold, carefully crafted visual identity is in many respects an extension
of her art, celebrating her Mexican heritage and countercultural ideals
while defying traditional notions of female beauty. Striking and
bursting with colour, her portraits resonate as much today as ever.

FLAME TREE PUBLISHING | The Art of Fine Gifts
6 Melbray Mews, London SW6 3NS, United Kingdom